Act Now!
5 Action Steps To Take Immediately To Move Your Business Forward

By Charlene L. Parlett, AAM, CPS

Copyright © 2017
Seamless Properties, LLC

Act Now! 5 Action Steps To Take Immediately To
Move Your Business Forward
Written By
Charlene L. Parlett

Copyright © 2017 Seamless Properties, LLC

All names, characters, businesses, places, events and incidents are either the products of the author's imagination or used in an illustrative manner only.

All rights reserved. No part of this book may be reproduced or transmitted in any form or by any means, electronic or mechanical, including photocopy, recording, or any information storage and retrieval system, without permission in writing from the author.

Library of Congress Cataloging-in-Publication Data
Parlett, Charlene L.1969 –
Act Now! 5 Action Steps To Take Immediately To
Move Your Business Forward/non-fiction/by Charlene L. Parlett
ISBN-13: 978-1545508817
ISBN-10: 154550881X
BUS060000 BUSINESS & ECONOMICS / Small Business
1. Non-Fiction, American I. Title.

Cover Illustration Copyright © 2017 by Seamless Properties, LLC
Book Design and Production by Createspace

Formatted and/or Printed in the United States of America

TABLE OF CONTENTS

Acknowledgements	1
Introduction – Why Act Now?	3
1. Strategic Planning	6
2. Quality Contracts	11
3. Social Media Skills	20
4. Priorities	33
5. Time Management	40
Moving Forward…	44
About	47

ACKNOWLEDGEMENTS

Writing a book is a massive undertaking. It requires diligence and constant focus. At times you doubt you have anything worth reading, even if you are the expert at what you do. That's why friends and family are so vitally important to the process. They provide you with encouragement and boost your confidence so you keep believing that this massive effort is worth it.

I must first acknowledge my children, Rachel and Ryan. They are my greatest cheerleaders.

I have a multitude of friends who provided a shoulder to cry on or a kick in my rear, depending on which one I needed in the past few years. You know who you are. Thank you.

I also want to acknowledge Ron and Minnie DePriest, John Kelly, Dr. Keith Johnson, and Drs. Timothy and Cindy Byler. These individuals continually provide me with devoted friendship, inspiration and motivation to do what I do. They are my personal mentors and leaders. John Kelly was the first man to reinforce in me that I had just as much ability as anyone to be successful in business. As a woman who was often the only female at the table this was a mental game-changer for me.

To all the small business owners out there who struggle to hang onto their dream - You are the inspiration for this book and for everything I do daily in my career. I hope that by reading this you find yourself moving forward.

INTRODUCTION

August in coastal Georgia - walking out your front door reminds you of opening the oven door to pull out a casserole. At night the air conditioner rarely cycles off, working hard to keep it somewhat comfortable in the house while still trying to keep the electric bill below heart attack range.

It's 2005 and my business partner and I have just quit our jobs to renovate a leased building. For the first time in both our lives we have zero income and huge outflow in security deposits, rent, utilities, building materials, labor, equipment and living expenses – all riding on the hopes and dreams that owning a business will bring us the financial and personal freedom we crave.

Expectation and excitement take turns swapping out with exhaustion and terror. What were we thinking? Every time we turn around something else needs fixed or a contractor wants a check. We've put all our savings, home equity loans, and a huge financial gift from my father into start-up capital, but it's dwindling away faster than we ever expected.

In the middle of a sleepless night I face the fear: What is the worse-case scenario? What if we fail miserably? Lose everything? The worse-case scenario is bad, really bad - but not devastating. I have friends and family that will not allow my family to go homeless or hungry. Bankruptcy is survivable and doesn't last forever. My previous employer made it clear that I always have a job waiting with them.

So I focus on the best case scenario. Incredible success! Multiple businesses! Financial freedom!

On September 1, 2005 I opened the doors on my first joint business venture. It was a lot like Grampa pushing me off the dock to learn how to swim. Those first years were spent treading water and looking for the shallows - that worked for a short period of time. Around the third year we realized there was a lot we needed to learn. The business had grown fast but was now stagnate. We needed people to help us learn the keys to success that have little to do with the actual work you perform or items you sell - the behind-the-scenes ownership stuff.

According to the Small Business Administration, over 80% of small businesses fail within the first 2 years and over 60% of those that survive fail within the next 5-10 years. Working with a business coach was the most important decision I ever made to keep that from happening to mine. That same successful business continues to be in operation today.

The experience of owning a small business and working with a business coach made me realize that my own calling was to help other business owners learn the same secrets to success that I did. As a small business coach, I work with service based business owners helping them thrive and not just survive.

I wrote this book based on the top five issues I've seen over and over as areas where small business owners need a hand-up in order to stay successful. I hope you will find it to be a valuable resource. The most important point is that you need to **ACT NOW!** on the areas in this book. It will do you no good to read it and forget about it. At the end of each chapter, create an action plan that works for your business. Don't wait – **ACT NOW!** You will be glad you did.

STEP 1
STRATEGIC PLANNING

"...a dream without a plan is just a wish..."
Katherine Paterson, Best-Selling Author

All small businesses start with a dream. Perhaps the dreamer is an automotive technician who sees how management treats customers and believes it's possible to do better. Maybe the dreamer is a corporate CEO who wakes up and realizes their calendar, priorities, and personal life is no longer their own as their job demands more and more from them. It could be a young person who grew up in a family of serial business owners who wonders how they can improve on what has already been built.

And so the dreaming begins. A picture of how things could be better. Better products. Better customer service. Better care of employees. The dream of freedom is a big part for that potential business owner: The freedom to innovate. Financial freedom (no one goes into business dreaming of being poor.) Freedom to control their own schedule. It looks so wonderful in our heads – but most people stop at the dreamer stage. It's easy to dream; putting a dream into action takes a lot more effort. It requires time, resources, education and commitment to a possibly slow and very expensive process.

The committed few who decide to put action to their dreams start with a business plan. They research the internet for basic outlines and templates. Most business plans are formatted to convince banks, creditors and investors to trust you with their money based on your experience and your "best guess" of how well your potential company will do financially. And while this is a good start, most business plans fall far short of an in-depth strategic plan for long-term growth and sustainability. Why? *Because you don't know what you don't know yet.* Until you have been in business a few years, you may not even know what questions you need to be asking yourself. And the first signs of this are often when you are standing there wondering why your business stopped growing.

My service business was in full swing for three years before we came to a screeching halt. Well, not exactly - we were still making money but not at the same rate. Operating expenses were growing faster than sales. We weren't booked solid so our technicians had time on their hands and that meant lost revenue. I realized quickly that we had outgrown our business knowledge base. We simply didn't know what we needed to do to grow anymore. I reviewed our business plan and there were no answers to be found. We started following the "spaghetti method" for growth – we tried pretty much every marketing idea that came our way and threw it on the wall to see what stuck. We tried adding all kinds of services that a salesperson promised us would bring in new customers. We wasted thousands of dollars in ineffective marketing and advertising efforts and unused products and equipment. Our end result: a few new customers and the ones we got were not our ideal customers.

About this time I was introduced to what real strategic planning meant when I was contacted by a business coach that specialized in service based businesses. I attended a 2-day workshop and by the end of it I realized what the gaps in my business were and began to understand why we weren't growing. *Heart and perseverance weren't enough anymore; we needed a strategic plan, education, and accountability to make changes as soon as possible.*

A strong strategic planning process is two-fold:

- Development of structure, clarity and processes for long term growth.
- Education and development of focused immediate action plans.

If all your time is spent on the first area, you'll get discouraged. Some immediate changes are needed in order to get momentum started.

The process for my business looked like this:

- **A detailed 12-step program** that would help us define our vision, focus, and guide decisions for the long-term future.
- Identifying the areas that needed immediate action to increase cash flow, customer retention and new customer acquisition.

I'll forewarn you - this is not an easy process. Defining who and what you want to be and writing it down are difficult. It requires saying a definitive NO to good things and a resolute YES to better things. Change is difficult, even when you know it's what you need to do. Think back on how challenging it is to change bad habits for most of us. Now envision trying to enforce those same changes on an entire company of employees, some who really don't want to make those changes. I could not have done so successfully and long-term without the accountability of my business coach. Knowing someone not only had my back but was willing to be the bad guy and help me enforce these necessary changes is an indisputable part of the continuing success.

If you read this and realize your business needs greater clarity, structure and processes in order to grow effectively, I encourage you to consider the Leaders Of Destiny® Program. The Leaders of Destiny® system is a guided, detailed 12-Step strategic planning program. For more information, please see the final chapter, **Moving Forward**.

For most of you reading this, the areas that need **immediate** action in your business are what the rest of this book is about. My goal is to give you at least a few gold nuggets in each session that you can start applying within the next 90 days to see noticeable improvements.

ACTION PLAN:

What 3 steps are you going to take within the next 30 days to implement what you learned in this chapter?

1._____

2._____

3._____

STEP 2
QUALITY CONTRACTS

"If you are building a culture where honest expectations are communicated and peer accountability is the norm, then the group will address poor performance and attitudes."
Henry Cloud, PhD – Best Selling Author & Change Agent

Don't skip over this chapter even if you hate paperwork; you'll thank me later...

During the course of owning a business you will have to deal with a lot of contracts. In this section I am going to talk about two very specific ones that are often neglected, by either lacking specific and important details, or not existing at all.

OPERATING AGREEMENT

Your operating agreement is part of your legal documentation when you form a Partnership, a Limited Liability Company (LLC), or a Corporation. If you started your business with a friend, family member or spouse, chances are you didn't include vitally important clauses and/or details. If you formed your LLC or corporation using a website rather than a good business contract lawyer, I PROMISE that you neglected making sure the following were clearly outlined:

- Members/Stockholders' process for sale of shares.
- Dissociation from and Dissolution of the legal entity (business).

Let me tell you why you didn't include these things (or at the very least left out vital details that will be needed if and when these situations occur): *You didn't want to believe they would ever happen.*

Why do couples continue to get married **without** a prenuptial agreement - despite the divorce rate teetering around 50% of all marriages? *Because when you are starting the journey of life (or business) together, you don't want to think that it's ever going to end.*

There are many reasons why a business partner or shareholder may need to sell their share in the business. It *could* be a breakdown in the relationship between the owners. It could also be that a financial hardship (such as personal bankruptcy or a serious health issue) occurs for one of the owners and they need cash now. It could be the desire to move closer to family, take care of an elderly parent, or any number of reasons why they need to have the financial and personal freedom that selling would provide.

Based on personal experience, I can tell you that it is MUCH EASIER to make decisions on how to handle a situation BEFORE it happens! In my case, what started out as an amicable divorce in which I thought we could continue as business partners quickly disintegrated into a hostile work environment and led to my decision to sell my share of the business. Unfortunately, the operating agreement did not specify how a conflict between members of the LLC and/or the specifics on how a sale of shares would be negotiated. The lack of specific details on how to proceed left me in a precarious position financially and personally. It resulted in the need to hire two lawyers and a mediator to avoid a court battle. It became an emotionally stressful and debilitating experience, resulting in a bad decision on my part and ignoring my lawyer's best advice. I walked away with about 40% of the value calculated by an independent third-party valuation. If the operating agreement had been better written, most of that turmoil could have been avoided.

DON'T WAIT! Take your LLC or corporate paperwork, specifically your operating agreement, to a qualified business contract lawyer and discuss these issues. Discuss options on how the business valuation should be calculated with a business valuation specialist (contract lawyers will include the agreed-upon valuation methodology into your operating agreement). PAY AN EXPERT to write these contracts and have all shareholders come to agreement *before* you need to. Don't assume (like I did) that everything will always work out the way you want it to. There are very few guarantees in life and even fewer in business.

In all cases, specific details of how the owners want a sale to occur should be in writing, so answer these questions:

- Is there a minimum required timeframe before shares can be sold? For example, must a shareholder or partner hold their shares for a minimum of 3 years?

- Does the other owner(s) get first right of refusal, or can any shareholder sell to anyone at any time?

- How will the shares be valued? Will the company request a business valuation report be prepared? What method of valuing the business will be used? Will there be a discount offered if the other owner(s) purchases the shares, rather than selling to an outside party?

- Will the seller require payment in full or be willing to offer seller-financing of all or part of the sale price? And if so, what are the terms?

- How will dissolution of the corporation be determined and handled?

Disclaimer: I am not a lawyer and every state has different laws governing this issue. Find a good quality business contract lawyer in your area.

EMPLOYEE CONTRACTS

"I'm a small business. I only have 2 employees. I don't need contracts – their paycheck is their contract!"

A coaching client shared with me this story that occurred before we started working together: soon after hiring a new office assistant, the new employee exhibited several personal issues that began to affect both her work performance and attendance. For three years the owner accommodated the employee's personal problems at the peril of the business, until a very public incident occurred that finally resulted in the employee being terminated for cause. The owner wanted to know what she could have done differently. My first response was to say, "I am surprised that she was employed that long, when you saw issues so early on. Were they addressed then? Was there a contract in place specifying expectations on attendance and work performance? Was each incident documented and discussed with the employee?" The answers, not surprisingly, were no – the most common response.

I'm guilty of this too – for years I had nothing in writing to hold employees accountable. I kept employees who were not producing good work on the payroll for way too long because I failed to correct them until I fired them. When an unemployment claim was filed, I had to scramble to make sure I could justify in writing why the employee was fired!

All of us have done this at least once. Business owners are some of the most compassionate people I know. We allow our hearts to override our better judgment and even direct evidence that someone who works for us isn't working out. We fail to directly address issues because we aren't sure what the proper way to address them is, or perhaps we don't want to embarrass the individual – or maybe we don't want to face the problem ourselves. *There is a not-so-fine line between providing a helping hand and enabling failure.*

One of the reasons small business owners struggle with the line between compassion and enablement is that we fail to provide clear expectations from Day One and hold team members fully accountable to what they agreed to when they were hired. **It is unfair and unreasonable to hold someone accountable without clear expectations - a detailed employment contract does this.** It is the guiding document for both employee and employer. When a team member goes above and beyond expectations, it should be publicly honored *and* *documented.* When they fall short, it should be privately discussed *and documented.* When you hold people accountable, you give them both the opportunity to thrive and the safety net not to fail. If they make multiple bad decisions, you now have the tools to remind yourself that sometimes your heart doesn't have the right answer, and that's ok. As a business owner you have to do what's best for the entire team. That's not always easy.

Here are the top 8 items I recommended clients include in an employment contract:

- Employee's Name.

- Start Date of Employment.

- Evaluation Date (I recommend a 3 day and a 30 day evaluation, and then a formal review at least annually).

- Starting Pay (and if there are specifically agreed-to increases at certain dates or milestones).

- Expected Days and Hours on Duty (including if the employee is expected to arrive early to prepare for opening or closing).

- Primary Duties: consider breaking down into daily and weekly duties as appropriate. If those duties include minimum required sales goals, billable hours, etc. that needs to be specified, including timeframes for achieving them.

- Other Duties: any other duties the employee may be expected to fulfill on an as needed basis.

- Benefits and when they become active (for example, if paid holidays start after 90 days of full-time employment).

An UPDATED contract should be created and SIGNED at any changes.

The point of a detailed employee contract is to provide clear communication between the employee and employer of all expectations – NOT rules of servitude. You and your new hire need to have in writing what each expects of the other – you need to make it clear what you want them to achieve, and they need to be clear on what the pay and benefits are for achieving success. You should have an employee contract reviewed by a Human Resources specialist in your state for any additional legal clauses required.

HANDBOOK

Do you have a team handbook that all employees must abide by? A document that spells out important information such as company-wide policies, benefits, hours, work standards, holidays, etc.? This goes into further detail about the expectations you have for every team member as well as all benefits, special privileges of being an employee, company wide policies, etc.

For a FREE editable Team Handbook sample template
Visit www.seamlesscoach.com

ACTION PLAN:

What 3 steps are you going to take within the next 30 days to implement what you learned in this chapter?

1._____

2._____

3._____

STEP 3
SOCIAL MEDIA SKILLS

*"These days, **social media waits for no one**. If you're LATE for the party, you'll probably be covered by all the noise and you might not be able to get your voice across. It could only mean that if you want to be heard by the crowd, you have to be fast; and on social media, that means you have to be REALLY fast."*
Aaron Lee – Social Media Guru

NOTE: The role and functionality of social media channels is constantly evolving. For the most up-to-date info, visit www.seamlesscoach.com

Let's start with the facts:

Google is the #1 Search Engine in the United States, not by a small margin but an ocean-wide lead;

The #2 Search Engine in the world is YouTube – and Google OWNS YouTube;

Unless your primary customer is over the age of 70 you are wasting your money paying for phonebook advertising - 84% of the population is looking for your goods and services through a smartphone screen;

Most of those smartphones have Google already locked and loaded.

I am very passionate about small businesses succeeding and I am shocked at how little most small business owners understand the importance of maximizing their online presence. This section will educate you on how to maximize the top social media sites for your marketing and advertising, no matter what you are selling. Let's start with the big guy:

Google My Business (aka Google Plus) – While Google Plus did not do well as an alternative social media platform to Facebook, Google smartly refocused its efforts to make it an important social media and advertising option for businesses by tying it in to the ranking and search engine program itself. You want to make sure your business is in the top 10 organic (i.e., unpaid) listings in a local search when your potential customer goes looking for what you sell.

Step 1: Claim Your Page. Making Google Plus work for you starts with claiming your Google Plus page. Unless your business is brand new or you have done nothing (and I mean zero effort) to have an internet presence, Google has probably already created a basic Google listing for you. You must "claim" that listing as belonging to you. Google will mail you a postcard with an activation code to the mailing address of your business. It takes approximately 10 days to receive the card and you have a limited number of days to follow the instructions on the card and activate your account. *While Google does not* *require you to have a Gmail account, I find it helpful to have one to speed up logging into my page. I also direct notifications for my page to it, along with any special offers from Google.*

Step 2: Accurate Information. After you claim and verify your Google Plus page, it's time to get some information in it. Make sure your location is accurate on the map – this feature is directly linked into GoogleMaps and customers will be frustrated if they follow it and you are not where the map says you are. Same thing with your phone number being accurate - most customers are pulling you up on a mobile device and want to be able to click and call. You can also add your company's website url if you have one.

Next is categories; you need to select categories (tags) that Google recognizes. You'll know if it is recognized if it comes up automatically when you start typing it. *This is an important part of how Google decides if it is going to bring you up in a search.*

Step 3: Introduction. Your introduction needs to be about your potential customer, not about you. They want to know what benefits they get from choosing you over your competitor. Survey your customers to see what THEY say is the reason they do business with you. My suggestion is to select 5-10 people to have coffee with and ask them about it. Then use those points as the heart of your intro. Don't overuse key phrases like "great customer service" – tell them why your customer service is amazing! What do you do differently that your customers say makes the difference? What do you offer that means a lot to them? It doesn't have to be different from the competition; sometimes it just means telling people you do it. Do you offer a peace of mind warranty? Loyalty rewards or discounts? Referral incentives? Lots of businesses do, but perhaps being made aware of it is the reason your customers come back.

Step 4: Reviews. It's possible that even before you claimed, verified and populated your page that you already had a review or two. Reviews on Google are VITALLY IMPORTANT and the number of reviews will affect how high you rank in a search. If you have reviews already, make sure you respond to them. YES, respond to every review! Be positive and polite at all times; even a bad review may have a grain of truth in it. If you dropped the ball say you are sorry they did not have a 5-star experience. Sometimes a customer's expectations are too high and you were never going to get a good review; you should still respond politely. The world is going to read how you reacted and judge whether they want to do business with you. No matter what, actively ask for reviews. Ask EVERY customer to leave a review. Create a card with a QR code that takes them right to your review page so they can submit a review from their smartphone. Have a prize drawing for the first 20 reviewers (positive or negative). Keep asking even after you have several; newer reviews carry more SEO weight than older ones. Fresh reviews show you are great at what you do and have a track record proving it.

To learn how to create a link for customers to leave a review
after you have created your GoogleMyBusiness page, visit www.seamlesscoach.com

Keep it up to date. Post regularly. Set up your blog to post a link update when you add a new blog post. We could spend the entire chapter just on Google, but if you get these 4 steps completed, you are on the right track. Let's move on.

Facebook Business Page – Who is on Facebook? While there is a lot of talk of teens and twenties stepping away from Facebook, a huge number of users in the 30 – 60 age range are on it multiple times a day. This goes across all genders, income levels, and regions of the US and the world. One of my favorite things about marketing with Facebook is that you can target your advertising dollars to ONLY the audience that you will get the biggest bang for your buck – who is YOUR target audience? In other words, picture the person you consider your BEST customer. Are they male or female? How old are they? What are their interests? What is their household income? When you can get that detailed, it makes a big difference on the return you will get on your marketing dollars. And when it comes to paid advertising, Facebook is still a bargain compared to your other options. Here's where to start:

Step 1: Page vs. Profile. If you are using a FB personal profile for your business (as in you created a profile with its own login and password just for it), FB will close you down when (not IF) they find out. This is against their guidelines. I know there are benefits to doing it that way, but it can get you banned from FB. You need to create a FB page from your personal profile. On your left sidebar, there is a CREATE PAGE button. Just follow the steps. You may not be able to complete all of it at once, but at least get it started and CLAIM YOUR LINK NAME! Make it the name of your business or close to it if what you want is already used. This is so important - people search for businesses, phone numbers and hours of operations through FB all the time – *why would I switch to Google if I am already browsing thru my FB feed?*

Step 2: Information. From left to right looking at your page you have a few things you need to add. I always recommend a logo for the profile picture, unless YOU are your logo. Next, a cover photo, something that adjusts well to wide screen and is not too busy. Even a stock image is a good option. Make sure you add your business address, phone number, and any additional important information asked for. Next, click on SETTINGS. Here you can add people to help manage your page – for example, your manager or business coach (hint, hint). On the far left click on PAGE again and it will take you back to your page. Here you can create your first post. I suggest a photo and a short, 1-line intro. Finally, right above the post section, you will see 3 dots. Click on it and invite friends and email contacts to LIKE your page. You will notice that you can only send invitations to people you are friends with on your personal profile.

IMPORTANT NOTE: Your customers have options when they LIKE your page – to ask for new posts to be at the top of their feed, to be notified when you post something new (as often as possible, that is the choice you WANT them to make!) or the default setting for LIKED business pages. Not everyone is aware of this change – be sure to ASK the people you invite to select Notifications or Top of Feed so they don't miss out on anything!

Step 3: Posts. You've now created a basic FB page for your business. Now we want to fill it with relevant posts. I strongly encourage photos, videos and always commenting before you post any link to an article or news item. This helps build content, but the more original content (as opposed to links), the more relevant your posts become to search engines. Take photos of your staff, your location, your happy customers, special sale items, delivering donations to a food bank or animal shelter – this is not the time to be shy about tooting your own horn. Let people know you have a vested interest in the success of your community and not just your business. Ask people to LIKE and SHARE your posts. Facebook decides whether or not your business posts will show up in someone's newsfeed based on the popularity, interaction and preferences of that post. A good way to make sure more of your business posts get seen is to like and share them on your personal news feed. Ask friends and family to do the same. If your employees are great team members, ask them to do the same. The more interaction, the more likely that the post will be put in the news feeds of everyone who liked your business page but chose the default option.

Step 4: Videos. A popular feature for Facebook posts is short video segments and LIVE video. Unlike posting a link to a Youtube® or Vimeo® video, in which all the person sees on their FB feed is a still picture and the link to follow, posting a video directly onto your FB page catches the eye because the movement is immediate. All your audience has to do is click to hear the audio and they're watching! Most free and for-a-fee video editing software already comes with a FB-formatting option; be sure to save the edited version SEPARATELY from your raw footage, as the FB formatting may not work across other social media platforms such as Google+, Twitter, and YouTube. Videos are most effective when they are short (less than 4 mins), entertaining, engaging, and fun. Let your clients and prospects see the human side of you and your team. Birthdays and anniversaries are just as important as highlighting new equipment or services added to enhance your customers' experience with you.

YouTube® Channel - Very few small businesses utilize YouTube® in their marketing plan. Why is that? I think the idea is a little intimidating. Maybe you think the video has to look professional and "perfect" - It's got to be creative and interesting, be in focus, have decent sound quality, use the right camera angles and background, and then take the time to learn how to edit it to clean up any mistakes… All of those ingredients do make for a great YouTube video, but all of them are not necessary every time to create something that your audience will enjoy watching. The real question is why aren't you making them? YouTube is the #2 search engine in the United States, remember! An active YouTube channel linked to your Google business page helps rank you higher in searches. Let's get started:

Step 1: Creating a YouTube Channel. You MUST have a Google account to have a YouTube channel. So go back and follow the steps in my previous blogs for setting up an account and a Google+ (also called Google My Business) page. It's important to create your business YouTube channel so that it is connected to your GoogleMyBusiness page.

For the link that will take you directly to how to Create A YouTube Channel, visit www.seamlesscoach.com

Following the link I provide is the fastest and easiest way to accomplish creating a channel. It includes links straight to the page on YouTube you will need to create a channel for your business. After you click the link, look for the Google+ page you created and click on it to create a channel (HINT: Don't accidentally create a channel that is not linked to your Google+ page. But if you do, it is easy to delete and start over).

Step 2: First Video. Don't let the first video be intimidating. A good quality cellphone, video camera or tablet will provide decent picture quality. My personal "must haves" are simple: 1) a tripod to hold the camera still, 2) a decent quality video recording device (I like to use an ipad personally because the person manning the camera has a large screen to view), 3) a decent microphone, either lapel based or free standing, that connects to your camera device for sound quality, and 4) a basic video editing program (which is often pre-loaded on PCs). Next, I highly recommend a script for your first video rather than winging it. You don't necessarily have to memorize word for word what you will say, but notes go a long way to keep you focused and make sure everything you want to convey in a short (3-5 mins max), entertaining way gets covered. Plus, Youtube SEO is best when a transcript is included of what is said in the video, so a script can be downloaded and help search engines find your content easier.

Step 3: Editing. The focus of your first videos should be content; a little editing is needed but the goal is to make videos and upload them so don't get overwhelmed. Keep it simple. A basic video editing program is plenty to start. Learn how to create and add an intro and outro with your contact info (business name, website, phone number, address), cut out long pauses or bloopers, and add a header or footer to the video. If you decide you really enjoy creating videos you can move on to learning how to add music, using a green screen, and special effects. There are plenty of learning resources, tutorials, and more online to learn how to use the video editing program you have. Although it is no longer supported by Microsoft many of us have Windows Movie Maker preloaded on our PC. Search online for a tutorial and you will be on your way!

Obviously we could go on and on – there are hundreds of social media sites. Different sites work better for different kinds of businesses; for example, if you are a boutique or restaurant, Pinterest or Instagram can be very effective. Others may find LinkedIn a great option. Keeping up with social media can be overwhelming and time consuming. Tools such as Hootsuite help you consolidate and manage multiple social media sites from one location. Depending on your budget it may be a good decision to hire a company to manage your social media content. This has become a very competitive market so the cost of these services is significantly lower than just a few years ago. Ask for LOTS of references before signing a contract with any company. Don't assume that a big marketing company is better – lots of small website development and SEO companies do fantastic work because they are able to focus their efforts on a smaller clientele base.

For a list of strategic business partners that I personally use for local search engine directory management, social media management, and website development, visit www.seamlesscoach.com

ACTION PLAN:

What 3 steps are you going to take within the next 30 days to implement what you learned in this chapter?

1._____

2._____

3._____

STEP 4
PRIORITIES

"Most of us spend too much time on what is urgent and not enough time on what is important."
Stephen R. Covey – Author and Consultant

Life gets very daily when you own a business. You can get in a routine that focuses on the everyday challenges until you find yourself drifting off course. It happens all the time. The best way to keep that from happening is to set priorities in your work and personal life and make a commitment to stick to them. BUSY-NESS IS THE ENEMY OF SUCCESS!

If you must choose between spending time with your spouse and children or making more money, choose to spend time with your spouse and children. Your family appreciates your hard work providing a good living for them – but a big house, new cars and the latest toys do not replace spending one on one time with them. You will not go to your death bed saying, "I wish I worked more."

A personal note: I used to criticize married friends who seemed to constantly run off for a weekend alone or date night. My attitude (and that of my spouse at the time) was "We don't need to do that kind of stuff." Walking through a painful divorce that turned hostile taught me how very wrong that thinking was. When all you do together is run the business and your household, your intimate life is in serious danger without focused, purposeful, prioritized effort. *Please, please, please don't repeat my mistake.*

In general, I recommend setting the following personal priorities:

- **Spouse/Partner** – At least 1 date night a week. Owning a business can be draining on a relationship. One on one time is how you refuel.

- **If You Are Single** – Commit to at least 1 night a week to do something fun and rewarding. Force yourself to have down time and enjoy life.

- **Children and Family** – Put special events into the calendar and work around them. Commit to being there for dinner/homework/bedtime at least 3 nights a week. Spend time with your parents too when possible.

- **Business** – We'll discuss in a moment.

- **Health and Wellness** – Don't underestimate how important your health is. I discuss this in depth in my sequel book, **Act Next!**

- **Volunteerism** – Make time to do something that allows you to feel good about your contribution to your community.

Setting Priorities in Your Business

As the owner, you MUST force yourself to see above the daily grind. If you "can't see the forest for the trees" then how are you going to plan for the future growth of your company?

Oh, you don't need to grow? Explain that to me - because anything that isn't growing is dying:

> If you are at max capacity and productivity with your current resources, a plan for growth will guarantee the RIGHT decisions to expand are made. However, if you continue to be "at max" without growing, how many times will you turn new business away before people stop trying to buy from you? Not very long…
>
> If you are just busy enough to pay the bills, what happens when operating expenses (rent, utilities, fees) increase, as they inevitably will? You must grow at least a few percentage points faster than inflation to break even…
>
> If you are in the red, prioritizing your next action steps could be the difference between being in

business a few years from now or closing your doors next month.

A business owner should commit a minimum 3-5 hours weekly to focus on the following:

- Long Term Strategic Planning (the vision for the future and how to achieve it);
- Leadership Development and Continuing Education (both yourself and your leadership team);
- Developing and Reviewing Effective Processes and Procedures (how you want things done);
- Clear Communication of Goals and Vision (letting the team know where you want to go and how);
- Branding/Marketing/Advertising/Networking (it's ultimately YOUR name that's on the line);
- Evaluation of Key Performance Indictors (the dashboard gauges of how your business is doing)

Most business owners are entrenched in the daily hands-on work of the business. It takes hiring the right people and putting forth a conscious effort on your part to transition out of that position. The best way to build better habits that will benefit your business long term is to find someone to partner with that will hold you accountable and help you learn what you need to learn to achieve these priorities. A business coach, consultant, or professional development group are all great options. Below is a testimonial about how a business coach changed an owner's life:

"I'd spent countless hours studying, researching, and learning from the best business and leadership minds I could find. I attended seminars, conferences and workshops and bought books, CDs, and training materials. I had a wealth of knowledge, a millionaire's lot of it, but I found myself struggling to move forward, make changes, and take the action that I knew I needed to in order to achieve the success I desired. I had a passion for it, a gas tank full of high octane fuel if you will, but I was stuck in neutral with the emergency brake on. **Then I met my first coach.**

They knew what it took to run a successful business – ACTION. It wasn't enough that I had a head full of information. I needed to take action on what I knew. And that is what my coach helped make happen. They were able to pinpoint precisely the areas holding my business back, and provided me with a roadmap - a strategic plan - to make changes that would shift me from neutral into overdrive. They kept me accountable to those changes. They encouraged me and challenged me.

And it worked! My profitability more than doubled – no, I am not exaggerating. My labor hours were booked. While my team was hesitant at first to make changes, when they saw the results of more money for themselves and a happier, more satisfying work environment, they embraced the changes.

A few years later I found a new coach, one prepared to take me to the next level. They had a similar approach, but took the time to draw out of me what I already knew and help me devise a plan to apply that knowledge and make it work for me. They gave me insight where I needed it, challenged me with "homework" and weekly meetings together, and forced me to face the tough areas that needed to be worked out to move ahead. AGAIN – fantastic results.

I know that if I had not reached out to these coaches, I would not have broken down the walls between my knowledge and action on my own. **There is something powerful about synergy and accountability, which is what they brought to the table.** Today, I am an absentee owner of a successful service industry business. I have happy, successful employees that are self-reliant. I can depend on them to fulfill their duties and provide great service to my customers in my absence."

ACTION PLAN:

What 3 steps are you going to take within the next 30 days to implement what you learned in this chapter?

1._____

2._____

3._____

STEP 5
TIME MANAGEMENT

*"It's not enough to be busy, so are the ants.
The question is, what are we busy about?"*
Henry David Thoreau – Author and Philosopher

This chapter is closely tied to your priorities. You will always make time for the activities and relationships you deem important (consciously or unconsciously). There is a ton of information online regarding time management that you can access, so let's focus on the following:

What are you spending your time on? You can't effectively make changes until you know what you are doing with your time now:

1. How many hours per week do you spend doing "technician" work? For example, if you own a heating and air conditional company how many hours are YOU doing installs, repairs and maintenance work? It's important to be honest and accurate about this.

2. How many hours do you spend in support of those "technician" activities? Such as driving to work sites, picking up and delivering supplies and materials, calling vendors to coordinate deliveries and parts, etc.?

3. How many hours are you spending on time-wasters and unimportant activities? In my

experience, most emails fall in this category, along with games, personal social media time, extra-long lunch breaks, etc...

4. How many hours do you spend in the management of personnel and Human Resources (HR) issues? This includes supervising, dealing with employee conflicts and work related issues, payroll, benefits – you get the idea.

5. How many hours do you spend on strategic planning? Marketing and advertising campaigns? Customer retention and acquisition program development? Creating Standard Operating Procedures (SOPs)? Reviewing Key Performance Indictors (KPIs) and evaluating changes required as a result of current KPI data? What about team building?

Keep a written log daily for a week or two (a notebook in your pocket works well, or a timelog in your smartphone). Based on my experience with hundreds of business owners, you likely spend 90-100% of your time on the first three and little to none on the 4th and 5th areas. *#5 is where you should be spending 70-90% of your time - because all or most of #1-4 can be delegated to someone else.* The owner's focus should be on the areas that affect the long-term success of the business, not the daily operations. The owner needs to keep their ear to the ground and be aware of what is going on daily, but they are most effective when they can see the business from a distance and into the future.

After you know what you are spending your time doing, determine if you already have someone working for you that you can delegate some of these areas. If you don't then perhaps it's time to plan your next hire around the goal of freeing your time up. It might be more beneficial to hire a great office manager than another technician, or an entry-level delivery driver or technical assistant. Hire to free up the maximum amount of time on your own schedule. I fully understand that you can't remove yourself from everything you currently do, but reducing your workload by even 5 hours a week can change your entire business model and increase both profitability and productivity.

ACTION PLAN:

What 3 steps are you going to take within the next 30 days to implement what you learned in this chapter?

1._____

2._____

3._____

Moving Forward

Congratulations! You made it to the final chapter of a business book. I know how difficult it was to find the time to commit to it and I am honored that you felt the information was worth setting aside part of your lunch hour, your bedtime reading, or even your bathroom reading for it!

I am passionate about helping small business owners succeed. I'm tired of the success rate of small business in the United States being less than 10% to the 10-year mark; many of those barely make ends meet or are being sustained by a second job. That's not how it should be. By including my personal stories, both successes and failures, I want you to see that I've been where you are and understand the joys and frustrations of owning your own business. I wrote this book to give you a hand-up and provide you with practical, bite-size steps you can take to increase sales, manage your time and people better, and keep you and your company on the right track to being wildly successful (and not another statistic.)

ACT NOW! does not attempt to provide a solution to all your business challenges, but if you apply what you learned from it, I promise you will begin to feel a sense of momentum, confidence and relief you haven't before. As a certified Master Business and Executive Coach, I get a great sense of purpose and significance from helping business owners find balance and achieve the goals they have set for themselves, both personally and professionally.

If after reading Act Now! you see how working with a business coach could help you get the financial and personal freedom you want out of your business, please contact us for a FREE one-hour consultation.

For more information on the Leaders of Destiny© Strategic Planning Program,
email *info@seamlesscoach.com*
Subject: LOD INFO

The sequel book, **ACT NEXT!** delves into the next 5 areas I see most business owners struggling with: Leadership Skills, Communication, Personal Health, Networking Effectively and Accountability. If you found **ACT NOW!** beneficial, I know you will love **ACT NEXT!**

To your success!
Charlene Parlett
Master Certified Executive & Business Coach
Helping Exceptional Professionals Become Extraordinary Business Leaders

FREE GIFT!

I'd like to invite you to get ongoing tips, ideas and education to move your business forward to higher levels of success. Visit www.seamlesscoach.com and click the button on the home page to opt in. I will send you a link to get your free gift, my 23-page report ***7 Huge Mistakes You Are Making As A Small Business Owner – How To Fix Them To Make More Money FAST!***

About Seamless Coaching

Seamless Coaching Service was established in 2006 to provide service based business owners and organizations with education and knowledge necessary for continuing professional success. Seamless Coaching Service is the premier coaching and consulting firm for individual career planning and service-based businesses, serving thousands through coaching, training, seminars, workshops and speaking engagements. Our company, staff and clients strive to live lives of abundance – financially, personally and professionally.

About Charlene Parlett

As an executive coach, published author and certified trainer, our founder and CEO Charlene Parlett is an expert at guiding business owners, corporate executives and managers to become successful leaders. She helps driven people achieve balance in their lives and floundering people find their drive. She has a gift for breaking down the walls between knowledge and action and puts people on the path to success. An expert in conflict resolution and business practices and processes, Charlene is a powerful and professional coach. Her specialties include leadership/soft skills, confidence building, marketing, strategic planning and assisting organizations in developing and implementing best practices. She has worked with coaching organizations to help them develop their own business coaching certification courses. With the publication of her two how-to success books **Act Now!** and **Act Next!** Charlene hopes to help even more business and non-profit leaders achieve their highest potential.

As marketing director of a multimillion dollar independent office supply and furniture company, she played a major role in doubling the company's gross sales by being one of the primary writers on their successful bid for both a state-wide and a federal world-wide government contracts. In 2005, she and her business partner built their service business from dream to delivery, so she understands the challenges businesses faced in real terms. Charlene is passionate about constantly improving on what is great to make it even better and instills that passion in others.

Connect With Us Through Social Media

Google
https://plus.google.com/+SeamlessCoachingService Hinesville

Facebook
https://www.facebook.com/SeamlessCoaching

LinkedIn
http://www.linkedin.com/pub/charlene-parlett-aam/1b/517/322/

Twitter
https://twitter.com/seamlesscoach

For more information on Seamless Coaching Service programs or to book Charlene to speak at your event, visit www.seamlesscoach.com.

Copyright and Trademark Information

This book is protected by U.S. and International copyright laws. The reproduction, modification, distribution, transmission, republication, or display of the content in this book is strictly prohibited without prior written permission from Seamless Properties, LLC. This book is for your use only. You may not give this book away or share it with others. Any trademarked names mentioned in this book are the sole property of their respective companies. None of these companies are affiliated with Seamless Properties, LLC in any way.

Earnings Disclaimer

The information you'll find in this book is to educate you. We make no promise or guarantee of income or earnings. You have to do the work, use your best judgment, and perform due diligence before using the information in this book. Your success is still up to you. Nothing in this book is intended to be professional, legal, financial and/or accounting advice. Always seek competent advice from professionals in these matters. We also recommend that you check all local, state, and federal laws to make sure you are in compliance when using this information. If you break federal, state, city, or other local laws, we will not be held liable for any damages you incur.

www.ingramcontent.com/pod-product-compliance
Lightning Source LLC
Chambersburg PA
CBHW061221180526
45170CB00003B/1095